Published in 2014 by The Rosen Publishing Group, Inc.
29 East 21st Street, New York, NY 10010

Photo Credits: **KEY** tl=top left; tc=top center; tr=top right; cl=center left; c=center; cr=center right; bl=bottom left; br=bottom right; bg=background

DSCD = Digitalstock; iS = istockphoto.com; MAY = Mayang.com; N_MI = NASA Missions; SH = Shutterstock; TPL = photolibrary.com

front cover bg N; **1**c N; **2–3**c ESO; **3**tc N; **4–5**bg N; **6**bc SH; cl TF; **6–7**br ESO; **7**tl TF; **8**cl ASM; c CBT; cr, N; bc TPL; **8–9**bg ESO; tc, tc N **9**c, c, cr, tr N; cl wiki; **10**c N; **11**bl, br, cr, tc N; tl USGS; **12**bc ASM; cr, tc N; **12–13**bc N; **13**br CBT; c, tc, tl N; **14**bl iS; c N; **14–15**c N; **15**br, cr N; **16**bl N; **17**bc, cl, cr, tr N; **18**bc N; **18–19**bc, bg N; **19**bc, br, N; **20**bc, cl, tc N; **21**bl, br, c, c, tl N; **20–21**bg ESO; **22**bc, br, cl N; **22–23**tc N; **23**bg ESO; bc, br, cr N; **24**bc iS; br N; **25**br, br, br, br, br, br, br, br, cl, cr, cr, cr N; cl, tc wiki; **26**bl N; br wiki; **27**br, br N; cl SPL; **28**bl CBT; bc, cr N; **29**cl iS; cl N; **32**bg ESO

Weldon Owen Pty Ltd

Managing Director: Kay Scarlett
Creative Director: Sue Burk
Publisher: Helen Bateman
Senior Vice President, International Sales: Stuart Laurence
Vice President Sales North America: Ellen Towell
Administration Manager, International Sales: Kristine Ravn

Library of Congress Cataloging-in-Publication Data

Close, Edward, author.
 Moon missions / by Edward Close.
    pages cm — (Discovery education: earth and space science)
 Includes index.
 ISBN 978-1-4777-6178-6 (library) — ISBN 978-1-4777-6180-9 (pbk.) —
 ISBN 978-1-4777-6181-6 (6-pack)
 1. Project Apollo (U.S.)—History—Juvenile literature. 2. Moon—Exploration—History—Juvenile literature. 3. Space flight to the moon—History—Juvenile literature. I. Title.
 TL789.8.U6A5249 2014
 629.45′4—dc23
                          2013023455

Manufactured in the United States of America

CPSIA Compliance Information: Batch #W14PK2: For Further Information contact Rosen Publishing, New York, New York at 1-800-237-9932

EARTH AND SPACE SCIENCE

MOON MISSIONS

EDWARD CLOSE

New York

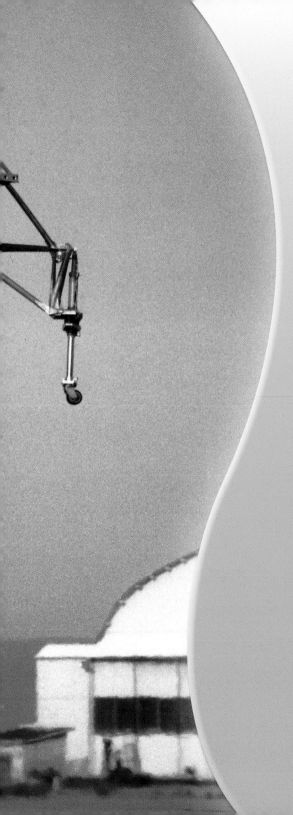

Contents

Moon Myths

The Moon has been associated with myths and legends for thousands of years. Since prehistoric times, people have gazed into the night sky and wondered how the Moon came to exist. What was this glowing round object shining high above us?

The Moon's amazing radiance suggests a feeling of magic and beauty, and this has led to its central role in the folklore of many cultures. The Sumerian people believed that souls of the dead traveled to the Moon, then descended to the underworld. The Greeks worshipped the Moon as the goddess of birth and fertility, while the Romans thought the Moon was the protector of their animals.

MOON MAPS

Galileo Galilei drew the first views of the Moon through a telescope. His drawings showed the major features we recognize today. Another early astronomer, Johannes Hevelius, published a map of the Moon in 1647, which showed the visible dark areas as watery seas.

Werewolves
One ancient legend claims that werewolves transform from humans into wolflike creatures under a full Moon in the night sky.

Selene the Moon goddess
The Greek Moon goddess Selene is known for her countless love affairs, particularly with the shepherd Endymion, with whom she had fifty daughters. The god Zeus placed Endymion into an eternal sleep so he would never grow old.

Johannes Hevelius

Eclipses

When the Moon passes directly between the Sun and Earth, a spectacular solar eclipse occurs. Day turns to night in seconds as light is blocked from reaching a few places on Earth. Lunar eclipses occur when Earth is directly between the Sun and the Moon, and Earth casts its shadow on the Moon. Lunar eclipses occur about once a year.

The Space Race

I n 1957, the Soviet Union launched the probe Sputnik 1 into orbit around Earth, causing shock around the world. The US did not want to be left behind and began preparations for their first space expedition. The space race had begun.

The Americans and the Soviets began programs of scientific research, but being the first nation to reach the Moon was a goal both countries wanted to achieve. The two countries were locked in the Cold War and saw the space race as a way of demonstrating their superior power.

1957
The Soviet's Sputnik 1, a small metallic ball, became the first artificial satellite to enter space and orbit Earth.

1957
Sputnik 2 carried the first animal, a dog called Laika, into orbit. Sadly, as there was no way to bring her back, she died in space.

1961
The Russian cosmonaut Yuri Gagarin became the first human in space, orbiting Earth in a rocket for 108 minutes.

1961
American president John F. Kennedy declared the US's goal of landing a man on the Moon before the end of the decade.

1962
The first American to orbit Earth was John Glenn, who circled the globe three times aboard the spacecraft Friendship 7.

ANIMALS IN SPACE

Before risking human lives, both the US and the Soviet Union used dogs, chimpanzees, and monkeys to journey into space. Most of these animals returned safely to Earth, proving humans could venture into orbit as well.

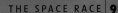

1963
Russian Valentina Tereshkova became the first woman in space, spending almost three days piloting Vostok 6.

1965
On June 3, 1965, Ed White became the first American to space walk outside his spacecraft.

1966
The Soviet Union's Luna 9 became the first spacecraft to achieve a soft landing on the Moon.

1966
The Lunar orbiter missions launched five spacecraft to photograph and map the Moon's surface.

1968
Apollo 8 was the first human expedition to leave Earth's orbit and venture to the far side of the Moon.

1969
The famous Apollo 11 landed the first humans, Neil Armstrong and Buzz Aldrin, on the Moon.

Flying bedstead
One experimental spacecraft vehicle used by NASA was the flying bedstead. Astronauts used this rocket-powered Lunar Landing Research Vehicle (LLRV) to practice taking off and landing the Lunar Module for the Apollo missions. Neil Armstrong was almost killed when he lost control and crashed his LLRV during a training exercise.

Astronaut Training

The first NASA astronauts were test pilots with jet aircraft experience. These brave men were required to have engineering skills and could be no more than 5 feet 11 inches (180 cm) tall because of the small spacecraft cabins. The pilots were used to flying in extreme conditions, which made them suitable for being NASA's first astronauts.

NASA training was not limited to just indoor simulators and test labs, however. Barren desert landscapes were used to practice moonwalking and rock sample collecting techniques. By the late 1960s, scientists, such as geologist Harry Schmitt, were also chosen as NASA astronauts.

Space Mission Survival

Before astronauts undertook a space mission, they needed to be trained in the skills that would help them survive in an emergency while in space or when returning to Earth.

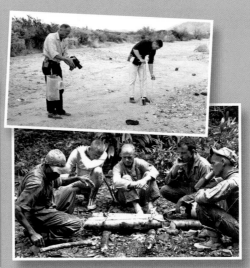

Identifying rocks
Geology training in Iceland, Canada, and the Grand Canyon, taught astronauts to identify rock types that would show evidence of how the Moon formed.

Moon landscape
Cinder Lake, in Arizona, was used to simulate a moonscape where astronauts could replicate exploring the surface of the Moon. Small craters were created by explosives and the astronauts could practice using their space suits, tools, and rovers.

Survival training
Astronauts carried out survival training in jungles, such as in Panama, in case they landed in remote areas when returning to Earth.

Wall walker
One NASA training method was to suspend astronauts sideways with cables and have them walk along a wall to simulate reduced-gravity conditions. This technique helped astronauts move around more easily when they were in space.

Parachute clothes
In the deserts of the western US, astronauts learned how to make clothing from parachute material. This would protect them from extreme heat if they landed in a hot, barren climate.

Extra time

The final countdown for an Apollo launch started at T minus 28 hours. The clock was stopped for scheduled holds to fix any technical problems that were encountered, so the countdown was actually longer than 28 hours.

T-28:00:00
Official countdown began

T-16:00:00
Rocket safety checked

T-11:30:00
Self-destruct rocket emergency devices installed

T-08:15:00
Loading of rocket fuel began

T-05:02:00
Flight crew medical exam

T-04:32:00
Flight crew had breakfast

T-03:57:00
Flight crew donned space suits

T-02:55:00
Flight crew arrived at launchpad

T-02:40:00
Flight crew boarded Command Module

Countdown

Apollo 11
This crest was worn by the Apollo 11 astronauts who first walked on the Moon.

Launch day arrived at Cape Canaveral, Florida, and the astronauts were ready to journey to the Moon. Mission controllers had to check every system during countdown to ensure the astronauts would be safe and the mission ran smoothly.

In the morning
With 5 hours until launch, the crew were checked by doctors. At T minus 4 hours and 30 minutes, the crew sat down for breakfast.

MISSION CONTROL

NASA's Mission Control is based in Houston, Texas. This is the team that gives final permission for the mission to go ahead at each critical stage. Dozens of people watched for warning lights to flash on computer screens, an indication of possible problems with a critical stage in the countdown.

Mission Control used a simple stopwatch to keep an eye on the countdown time.

Getting dressed
At T minus 4 hours, the astronauts were helped into the space suits they would be wearing for the launch.

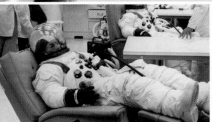

Ready for boarding
At T minus 2 hours and 40 minutes, the astronauts were ready to board the Command Module and prepare for liftoff.

T-01:55:00
Mission Control center link to spacecraft checked

T-00:15:00
Spacecraft switched to internal power

T-00:06:00
Space vehicle final status checked

T-00:03:10
Automatic launch sequencer system activated

T-00:00:50
Rocket switched to internal power

T-00:00:09
Engine ignition began

T-00:00:02
All engines were running

T-00:00:00
Liftoff!

At the launch pad
At T minus 3 hours, the astronauts arrived at the launchpad and took an elevator to the top of the launch tower.

Careful monitoring
Computers were used to monitor the crew, spacecraft, and rocket systems at the launchpad.

Liftoff

Thousands of spectators from all over the country gathered at Cape Canaveral, Florida, and millions of people around the world watched on televisions as Apollo 11 prepared for liftoff on July 16, 1969.

At T minus 9 seconds before launch, the Saturn V rocket engine ignition sequence began. The powerful thrust gradually built up and, at T minus 3 seconds, the engines reached full power. At T minus 2 seconds, the hold-down latches released the rocket from the tower, and at T minus 0, there was liftoff! The Saturn V rocket rose from the launchpad and, after 12 seconds, cleared the tower and headed toward space. Apollo 11 was headed for the Moon!

Hot ticket
Some lucky people had access to NASA's VIP viewing area for the Apollo 11 launch. These tickets became precious reminders of this once-in-a-lifetime event. Today, a full-size Saturn V launch vehicle replica can be seen at the Kennedy Space Center in Florida.

A POWERFUL BLAST

At more than 360 feet (110 m) high and 32 feet (10 m) in diameter, with a total mass of 6.6 million pounds (3 million kg) and producing 7.5 million pounds (3.4 million kg) of thrust at liftoff, the Saturn V is the biggest and most powerful rocket ever built. The force of the rocket was powerful enough to lift 500 elephants off the ground.

The Saturn V churned out more power than the equivalent of 85 Hoover Dams.

Capturing the occasion

Dozens of cameras were placed around the launch site, including one at the very top of the rocket. These remote cameras recorded video footage and photographed the launch from places that would have been far too hot for humans to be.

Mass appeal

Spectators camped for days to get a chance to view the Apollo 11 launch, positioning themselves up to 12 miles (19 km) from Cape Canaveral. Special guests could watch the liftoff from a grandstand much closer to the action.

Team effort

A team of hundreds of technicians working in the Kennedy Space Center at Cape Canaveral made sure the Saturn V safely cleared the launch tower.

1

Liftoff
The three-stage Saturn V rocket launched into orbit from Cape Canaveral, Florida. The Command, Service, and Lunar modules were positioned at the top of the rocket as it blasted into space.

2

Translunar injection
The first and second stages of the Saturn V rocket crashed back down to Earth. After one orbit of Earth, the third-stage engine ignited and boosted the astronauts toward the Moon.

Traveling to the Moon

I n 1961, when President Kennedy boldly set the goal that the US would land on the Moon before 1970, engineers had very little experience in launching humans into space. No one really knew the best way to land someone on the Moon.

Scientists eventually decided that the two-spacecraft method was the best approach, and preparations began. As it happened, this method worked extremely well and was used for all NASA Moon missions.

Transposition and docking

Crew detached the combined Command/Service Module from the spacecraft and combined it with the Lunar Module. The discarded third stage fell away.

Lunar orbit insertion

After three days, the Service Module's main engine slowed the spacecraft and it entered orbit around the Moon.

Descent to the Moon

Two astronauts entered the Lunar Module, which separated and landed on the Moon. The third astronaut observed from the Command/Service Module above.

Ascent stage liftoff

The astronauts returned to the Lunar Module and blasted off from the Moon's surface. The bottom half remained on the Moon.

Re–docking in lunar orbit

The top of the Lunar Module re-docked with the Command/Service Module and the astronauts moved back into the Command Module. The remaining Lunar Module was discarded and crashed to the Moon.

Transearth injection

The Service Module's main engine could now be ignited and the three astronauts blasted away from the Moon, back toward Earth.

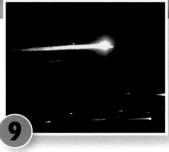

Reentry

Approaching Earth, the Command Module separated from the Service Module. Both reentered, but only the Command Module, with its heat shield, survived the extreme heat.

Splashdown

The Command Module descended through Earth's atmosphere and parachutes opened to slow its fall. The three astronauts, inside their spacecraft, splashed down into the Pacific Ocean and were picked up by a navy ship.

Apollo 11

The Eagle has landed! On July 20, 1969, one of the most dramatic events in the world's history occurred—man set foot on the Moon. Millions of people around the world watched closely as Neil Armstrong and Buzz Aldrin guided their Lunar Module, *Eagle*, to the Moon's surface. With just 20 seconds of fuel left, Armstrong safely touched the Lunar Module down in the Sea of Tranquility.

The Apollo 11 mission fulfilled President John F. Kennedy's goal of reaching the Moon by the end of the 1960s. As Neil Armstrong stepped off the Lunar Module onto the Moon's surface for the first time, he famously stated, "That's one small step for man, one giant leap for mankind."

First steps
Neil Armstrong was the first astronaut to climb out of the Lunar Module and set foot on the Moon. He was closely followed by a second astronaut, Edwin "Buzz" Aldrin. A third astronaut, Michael Collins, stayed in the Command Module and orbited the Moon.

Touchdown
As the Lunar Module descended toward the Moon's surface, Armstrong realized the autopilot controls were guiding them toward a field of large boulders. Thinking quickly, he took control of the Lunar Module and managed to navigate safely to a flatter landing surface. Despite a few hair-raising moments, they had done it.

UNITED STATES

A proud moment
After exploring their surroundings for a short while, Neil Armstrong and Buzz Aldrin erected the American flag on the Moon's surface. This act was repeated on future Apollo missions to the Moon. The footage was captured for people to watch back on Earth by a small black-and-white television camera attached to the outside of the Lunar Module.

Media sensation
The Apollo 11 Moon landing made headlines around the world. Most people alive in 1969 can still remember where they were when Apollo 11 touched down on the Moon.

Lunar landscape
Neil Armstrong ventured 200 feet (60 m) from the Lunar Module to photograph the landscape around the landing site.

Famous footprint
Buzz Aldrin famously photographed his own footprint so the lunar soil's properties could be identified. His boot left a clear outline in the Moon dust.

Must not forget
Neil Armstrong had a checklist of tasks to complete printed on the cuff of his space suit. This was so he would not forget to perform any experiments on his moonwalk.

Exploration

Once Neil Armstrong had safely stepped onto the Moon's surface and could freely move around, he began to explore the surrounding environment. Buzz Aldrin joined his crew member on the Moon 20 minutes later. The astronauts' tasks were to collect rock and soil samples, take photographs, and set up research equipment that would provide valuable data for scientists back on Earth.

1

Parachutes open
Three parachutes opened after the Command Module's fiery reentry into Earth's atmosphere.

Splashdown

The final stage of the Apollo 11 Moon mission was very dangerous. The Command Module entered Earth's atmosphere at a staggering 24,500 miles (39,500 km) per hour. One small mistake as the Command Module hurtled toward Earth and it could have burned up from the extreme heat, or hit the ocean too hard for the astronauts to survive.

2

Module slows
The parachutes slowed down the Command Module as it approached the ocean.

3

Module floats
Three large balloons inflated to keep the Command Module on the ocean surface.

Helping hand
After splashdown, the Command Module capsule floated upright on the surface of the ocean. Navy divers from a nearby aircraft carrier helped the astronauts exit the capsule and climb into safety baskets. The astronauts were then hoisted from the ocean by a helicopter and taken to the waiting ship.

Back to Earth
The Command Module was the only part of the spacecraft that returned to Earth intact. Its heat shield prevented it from melting, but the capsule was scorched brown from the extreme heat.

MOON GERMS

Scientists initially worried the astronauts might catch dangerous germs from their journey to the Moon. As a precaution, they were kept in isolation for two weeks after their return. This process was soon abandoned for future missions.

Astronauts are quarantined from President Richard Nixon.

After Apollo 11

The Apollo missions after Neil Armstrong and Buzz Aldrin first set foot on the Moon became more adventurous. There were five successful Apollo missions after Apollo 11. The Apollo 14 astronauts used a tool cart to collect Moon debris from an impact crater. Apollo 15 used a Lunar Rover to explore the Moon's mountainous regions. In 1972, the Apollo 17 astronauts used a Rover to travel nearly 5 miles (8 km) from their Module. This was the only Apollo mission with a scientist on board.

There were three more Moon landings planned as part of the Apollo program, however, these were cancelled as NASA had to cut costs. The six successful Apollo missions provided scientists with rock and dust samples to study in laboratories back on Earth.

Lunar Rover
Later Apollo missions used Lunar Rovers to explore the Moon's surface. The Lunar Rovers were equipped with wire-mesh wheels which provided good traction, four-wheel drive, four-wheel steering, and a television camera with an antenna attached.

Space tools
To collect rock and dust samples, astronauts used rakes to sift for small rocks and tongs to pick up rocks from tight crevices. Flipbook pages were used to identify the correct camera settings for space photography.

Rake

Tongs

Flipbook

Distance traveled on the Moon

This graph shows the total distance the astronauts traveled on the Moon by walking, using a hand-pulled cart, or driving a Lunar Rover.

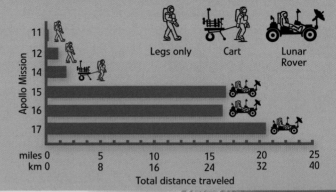

Legs only	Cart	Lunar Rover

Apollo Mission: 11, 12, 14, 15, 16, 17

miles 0   5   10   15   20   25
km 0   8   16   24   32   40

Total distance traveled

Low-gravity jump

The Moon has only one sixth of Earth's gravity. This very low gravity allowed astronauts to bounce in long strides across the Moon's surface.

SPACE SOUVENIRS

Astronauts left many souvenirs behind after they had returned from their moonwalk. The Apollo 11 crew left a gold olive branch symbolizing peace, while others left personal messages such as plaques and photographs dedicated to friends and family. These souvenirs will probably lie undisturbed on the Moon's surface for thousands of years.

Apollo 15's memorial plaque

Charlie Duke's family photograph

Apollo 13

The astronauts on the Apollo 13 moon mission had just finished filming a live television broadcast back to Earth, when a loud bang was heard and the oxygen and power meters fell to zero. An oxygen tank had exploded in the Service Module and damaged the spacecraft. As the tension climbed inside the spacecraft, hundreds of NASA staff went into action to work out how the crew could survive onboard. The crippled Command Module was shut down, as the astronauts made the four-day trip back to Earth in the tiny Lunar Module.

Houston, we've had a problem here.

JACK SWIGERT, COMMAND MODULE PILOT, APOLLO 13, APRIL 13, 1970

The Apollo 13 mission launched from Cape Canaveral in Florida on April 13, 1970. On board were the astronauts Jim Lovell, Fred Haise, and Jack Swigert.

An oxygen tank exploded on the journey to the Moon.

The astronauts fired the Lunar Module engine, normally used for landing on the Moon.

The astronauts looped around the Moon and turned toward Earth.

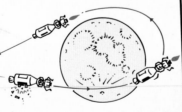

The tiny Lunar Module began to make the slow four-day journey back to safety.

The Command Module was powered up on its batteries and reentered Earth's atmosphere.

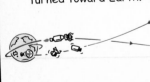

The astronauts splashed down safely and Mission Control celebrated their "finest hour" in Houston. Their tireless work had helped save the astronauts' lives.

The Apollo Program

The NASA Apollo Moon program began in the early 1960s. During this time there were six successful human Moon landings. The Apollo program has been hailed as one of America's finest achievements and brought great pride to the nation and the world.

UNMANNED

APOLLO MISSION: 5

DATE: January 1968

KEY FEATURE: To test the Lunar Module's ascent and descent engine systems

SUMMARY: An unmanned test flight of the Lunar Module

ORBITS

APOLLO MISSION: 7, 8, 9, 10

DATES: October 1968–May 1969

KEY FEATURE: First manned Apollo missions

SUMMARY: First orbit of Earth by Apollo 7, and first orbit of the Moon by Apollo 8.

DISASTER

APOLLO MISSION: 1

DATE: February 1967

KEY FEATURE: Intended as the first manned Apollo mission

SUMMARY: All three astronauts were killed by fire in a pre-launch test of the spacecraft.

LANDINGS

APOLLO MISSION: 11, 12, 14, 15, 16, 17

DATES: July 1969–December 1972

KEY FEATURE: First Apollo missions to land on the Moon

SUMMARY: Six missions were conducted, ending with Apollo 17, which was the last manned mission to the Moon.

LAUNCHES

APOLLO MISSION: 2, 3, 4, 6

DATES: 1962–1968

KEY FEATURE: Test launches of rocketsand spacecraft

SUMMARY: No crew were aboard in the testing stage of the Apollo program.

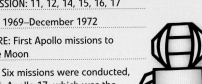

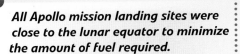

All Apollo mission landing sites were close to the lunar equator to minimize the amount of fuel required.

Revisiting the Moon

After the final Apollo mission in 1972, Moon travel was ignored for many years as the US and Soviet Union explored other planets and developed space stations instead. No spacecraft ventured to the Moon between 1976 and 1990.

In recent years, there has been a revived interest in lunar exploration, with Japan, China, and India all launching space probes to the Moon. Future lunar exploration in the US is part of NASA's Constellation Project, with a new Ares V rocket to launch the new Altair Lunar Lander into orbit around Earth.

Lunokhod 2 (1973)

Lunokhod 2 was the second of two unmanned Lunar Rovers landed on the Moon by the Soviet Union. It arrived aboard the spacecraft Luna 21. Mission Control guided the vehicle from Earth on a 23-mile (37-km) journey to collect images of the lunar surface.

Japan (2007)

Selene was the second spacecraft launched by Japan into lunar orbit. It orbited the Moon for one year and eight months, eventually crashing into the Moon's surface in June 2009. Scientists used data collected by Selene to study the Moon's geological evolution.

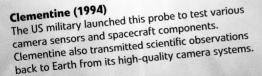

Clementine (1994)

The US military launched this probe to test various camera sensors and spacecraft components. Clementine also transmitted scientific observations back to Earth from its high-quality camera systems.

NASA Lunar Reconnaissance Orbiter (2009)

The objective of this orbiter was to create a 3-D map of the Moon, search for ice at the Moon's poles, and return high-resolution photographs that showed small details of the Moon's surface, such as the landers and rovers left by the Apollo missions.

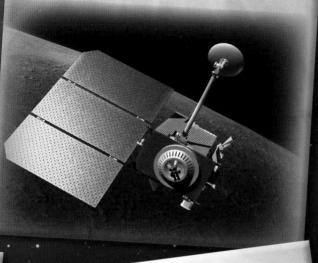

GLOBAL MOON MISSIONS

With 37, the US is the country that has launched the most missions to the Moon. Their nearest rival is Russia, which has launched 29 missions.

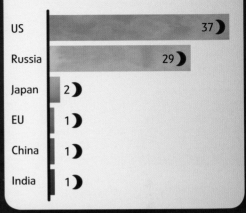

US	37
Russia	29
Japan	2
EU	1
China	1
India	1

Orion (future)

The US had plans to use the rocket Ares 1 to launch the Orion crew capsule, which would have docked with the Altair Lunar Lander and head to the Moon in the year 2020. NASA's Moon project has been cancelled, but the Orion might be used for other projects in the future.

Future Moon rover (future)

Aboard the spacecraft of the next Moon mission may be high-tech Lunar Rovers. These large, pressurized vehicles will be able to travel farther than ever before, allowing astronauts to explore craters, mountains, and canyons on the Moon's surface.

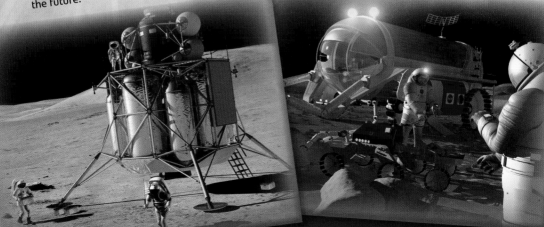

Moon Facts

Making craters
Craters are made when a meteor, asteroid, or comet collides with the Moon, blasting a huge hole in the surface.

1 Vaporizing
When an object impacts the Moon's surface, the object and surrounding rocks are vaporized.

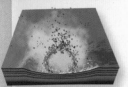

2 Cooling
The vaporized rock flies into space where it cools and rock fragments then fall back to the Moon.

3 Colliding
The crater formed is a circular shape, even if the object collides at an angle.

Highlands
Much of the Moon's surface has been impacted by meteors and asteroids for billions of years. These craters have formed bright highlands stretching as far as the eye can see. Some craters are up to 185 miles (300 km) wide.

Lava rock
This is formed from cooling lava.

Precious rocks
These are stored in airtight containers.

Moon rocks
The Apollo astronauts collected more than 2,400 samples of Moon rocks and dust from their Moon explorations. Moon rocks have been closely studied by scientists and are more precious than gold or diamonds.

Men's high jump
Earth record is 8.04 feet (2.45 m). The equivalent Moon record would be almost 50 feet (15 m).

Men's javelin
Earth record is 323 feet (98.5 m). The equivalent Moon record would be about 2,000 feet (600 m).

Women's long jump
Earth record is 24.67 feet (7.52 m). The equivalent Moon record would be 150 feet (46 m).

Earth
90 pounds (40.8 kg)

Moon
15 pounds (6.8 kg)

Weight loss

The Moon has six times less gravity than Earth does. So, whatever your weight is on Earth, you would weigh one sixth of that if you were standing on the Moon.

Hard lunar crust

Light rocky mantle

Small iron core

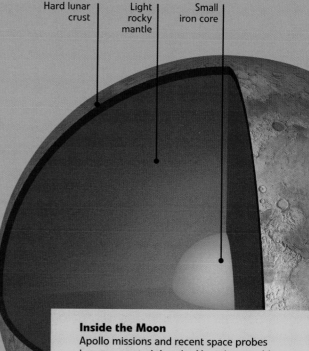

Moon temperature

In just a few short steps, the temperature can change from intense heat when in direct sunlight, to freezing cold in areas of constant shadow. Space suits protect the astronauts from these extreme conditions.

1 Sunlit surfaces can become extremely hot.

2 Surfaces in the shade are icy cold.

Inside the Moon

Apollo missions and recent space probes have suggested that the Moon has a cold, hard crust that lacks any dense metals. There is no magma activity beneath the Moon's surface.

Glossary

antenna
(an-TEH-nuh)
An electrical device used to send and receive radio and television signals.

Apollo (uh-PAH-loh)
A NASA space program launched in the early 1960s, with the goal of reaching the Moon.

asteroid
(AS-teh-royd)
A small, rocky, celestial body that orbits the Sun.

astronaut
(AS-truh-not)
A human space traveler.

atmosphere
(AT-muh-sfeer)
A thin layer of gases held in place around a moon or planet by its gravity.

comet (KAH-mit)
An object made of rock and ice that travels in long orbits around the Sun.

command module
(kuh-MAND MAH-jool)
The part of an Apollo spacecraft that contained the crew and main controls, and was used as the reentry vehicle.

core (KOR)
The central region of a planet.

cosmonaut
(KOZ-muh-naht)
The Russian word for a person who goes into space.

crater (KRAY-tur)
A circular pit caused by a comet or meteorite colliding with the surface of a planet or moon.

crust (KRUST)
The outer, rocky layer of Earth and other terrestrial planets.

debris (duh-BREE)
Broken, scattered remains or rubble.

geology (jee-AH-luh-jee)
The science that studies the history and formation of rocks.

gravity (GRA-vih-tee)
The invisible force that pulls everything toward the center of a planet.

launchpad (LAWNCH-pad)
The base from which a spacecraft positioned on its rocket is propelled into space.

lava (LAH-vuh)
Molten rock that flows from a volcano during an eruption. It is formed in the interior of a planet.

liftoff (LIFT-of)
The start of a rocket's flight from its launch pad.

lunar (LOO-nur)
Used to describe things to do with Earth's Moon.

lunar eclipse
(LOO-nur ih-KLIPS)
A shadowing of the Moon, as viewed from Earth, caused when our planet passes between the Sun and the Moon.

lunar highlands
(LOO-nur HY-lundz)
Mountainous regions of the Moon's surface.

Lunar Rover
(LOO-nur ROH-vur)
The carlike vehicle used by Apollo astronauts while exploring the Moon's surface.

mantle (MAN-tul)
The interior region of a planet or other solid body that is below the crust and surrounds the core.

mission control
(MIH-shun kun-TROHL)
The team in charge of managing a NASA space mission during the flight.

moon (MOON)
A natural satellite that orbits a planet.

Moon rocks
(MOON RAHKS)
Rocky materials found on the Moon's surface.

NASA (NA-suh)
The National Aeronautics and Space Administration, a US agency in charge of all government space programs for the US.

orbit (OR-bit)
The path that one celestial object takes around another celestial object because of the gravitational force between them.

quarantine
(KWAR-un-teen)
When people are put in isolation for a period of time to prevent the spread of germs and disease.

reentry
(ree-EN-tree)
The return of a spacecraft into Earth's atmosphere.

rocket (RAH-kit)
A craft propelled by the combustion of fuel and oxygen held onboard.

satellite (SA-tih-lyt)
Any object in space that orbits another object. Satellites can be man-made or natural.

Saturn V (SA-turn FYV)
A launch rocket that was used by NASA during the Apollo space program.

Service Module
(SUR-vis MAH-jool)
The part of the Apollo spacecraft that carried the engine, thrusters, electrical supply, and oxygen. It was discarded before the Command Module reentered Earth's atmosphere.

solar eclipse
(SOH-lur ih-KLIPS)
When the Moon passes in front of the Sun, blocking sunlight to a tiny portion of Earth's surface.

space probe
(SPAYS PROHB)
A man-made spacecraft designed to explore beyond Earth's orbit.

space station
(SPAYS STAY-shun)
An orbiting spacecraft designed to support human activity for an extended time.

space suit (SPAYS SOOT)
Protective clothing and equipment designed to keep humans alive and comfortable in space.

Index

Websites

Due to the changing nature of Internet links, PowerKids Press has developed an online list of websites related to the subject of this book. This site is updated regularly. Please use this link to access the list:
www.powerkidslinks.com/disc/moon/